othing is more beautiful than the miracle of marriage. Its beauty lasts a lifetime when two people care so much that they love each other forever.

— *Regina Hill*

Happy Anniversary!
Day & Chris
Lots of love always —
Tony & Deb

Blue Mountain Arts®
Bestselling Books

By Susan Polis Schutz:
To My Daughter, with Love, on the Important Things in Life
To My Son, with Love
I Love You

Is It Time to Make a Change?
by Deanna Beisser

To the Love of My Life
by Donna Fargo

100 Things to Always Remember... and One Thing to Never Forget
Chasing Away the Clouds
For You, Just Because You're Very Special to Me
To the One Person I Consider to Be My Soul Mate
by Douglas Pagels

Being a Teen ...Words of Advice from Someone Who's Been There
by Diane Mastromarino

girls rule ...a very special book created especially for girls
by Ashley Rice

A Lifetime of Love ...Poems on the Passages of Life
by Leonard Nimoy

Anthologies:
42 Gifts I'd Like to Give to You
Always Believe in Yourself and Your Dreams
A Daughter Is Forever
For You, My Daughter
Friends for Life
I Love You, Mom
I'm Glad You Are My Sister
The Joys and Challenges of Motherhood
The Language of Recovery ...and Living Life One Day at a Time
Life Can Be Hard Sometimes ...but It's Going to Be Okay
May You Always Have an Angel by Your Side
Take Each Day One Step at a Time
There Is Greatness Within You, My Son
These Are the Gifts I'd Like to Give to You
Think Positive Thoughts Every Day
Thoughts to Share with a Wonderful Teenager
To My Child
With God by Your Side ...You Never Have to Be Alone

MARRIAGE
Is Forever

A Blue Mountain Arts® Collection
About the Lifelong Journey
of Two People in Love
Edited by Gary Morris

Blue Mountain Press™
Boulder, Colorado

We wish to thank Susan Polis Schutz for permission to reprint the following poems that appear in this publication: "Marriage Is Two People Sharing Everything in Life" and "Together in marriage...." Copyright © 1988, 1991 by Stephen Schutz and Susan Polis Schutz. All rights reserved.

Library of Congress Control Number: 2002111341
ISBN: 0-88396-693-X

ACKNOWLEDGMENTS appear on page 64.

Certain trademarks are used under license.

Manufactured in China.
Second Printing: 2003

♻ This book is printed on recycled paper.

This book is printed on fine quality, laid embossed, 80 lb. paper. This paper has been specially produced to be acid free (neutral pH) and contains no groundwood or unbleached pulp. It conforms with all the requirements of the American National Standards Institute, Inc., so as to ensure that this book will last and be enjoyed by future generations.

Blue Mountain Arts, Inc.

P.O. Box 4549, Boulder, Colorado 80306

Contents

Marriage Is Forever

When two people join together and bond their lives forever because they are certain they have something special that will make their marriage last... this is the first act of faith.

Upon this act of faith, these two people will build a life. And as long as their determination stays with them, this life will always be their hope, their dream, their truth, their being, their inspiration, and their source of strength.

Through their life together, they will hurt and laugh. Together, they will feel all of life's ups and downs. They will learn and grow through trial and error. The lessons will show them the meaning of true love and the difference between a love that lasts and one that just gives up.

These two people will face each failure together and discover the strength to go on. They will encourage each other's dreams and forgive each other's faults.

Through a labor of love, these two will become as one — fighting against the odds and ultimately creating a marriage that will grow into an infinite love.

— Regina Hill

May Your Marriage Be Blessed with Love, Friendship, and Faith

arriage is based on love.
Love that looks at you and
only sees beauty.
Love that understands you
and wants you to be happy.
Love that hurts when you do,
that soothes your aching body
and heals your broken heart or spirit.

Marriage is based on friendship.
It's two people committed to sharing
an intimate relationship
and who are friends as well as lovers.
It's having a friendship filled
with laughter, hugs,
and playfulness.
A friendship that stands through
each trial and problem.
A friendship that is unconditional
and doesn't waiver or end.

It's based on friendship that guarantees
    there is someone who is
    always there for you,
someone's hand you can always hold,
someone you can trust.

Marriage is built on faith.
Faith that your marriage will last forever
and that nothing can ever
    come between you.
Faith that though marriage is hard work,
you'll both be willing to listen, to care,
    to try to understand,
and to accept instead of trying
    to change each other.
Faith that you've made the right choice
and have found the love of your life,
and that your lives will be filled with
all the happiness they can hold.

— Barbara Cage

"The Marriage Poem"

Being married is the most wonderful thing that can happen to two people in love ❧ A marriage is a caring commitment to making a miracle last forever ❧ It truthfully whispers the words, "I don't know what I'd ever do without you" ❧ It joyfully says, "I want you to be there in all my tomorrows" ❧ And it sings the praises of sharing life, as husband and wife, sweetly and completely together ❧

A marriage is opening the door to all the good things and best wishes around you ❧ A marriage is opening your hearts to the wonders within you ❧

A marriage is a promise to stay together, to dream together, to work on whatever needs attention, to keep love fresh and alive, and to continue to bless the beauty of your lives ❧ A marriage is reaching for the wishes you both want to come true, and remembering the priceless smiles that come from hearing "I love you" ❧

A marriage is one of life's most wondrous blessings ❧ It involves taking the words of two life stories and weaving them together on the same pages ❧ Every year, in a thousand special ways, the words that will be written in this remarkable story will reflect the strength and the joy and the love that rises above any trials and sorrows ❧ A marriage is the precious, reassuring comfort of having a kindred soul care about your day, every day and each tomorrow, your whole life long ❧

A marriage is the making of a blessed home that seems so meant-to-be... between a special woman and a special man ❧ A marriage is a beautiful journey along life's road with two people smiling as they go, lovingly... hand in hand ❧

— Douglas Pagels

Cherish the Gift You Have in Each Other

You have a special gift
in each other —
one that could never be replaced
or shared with anyone else.
This is one gift you can open
    every day of your lives together
and always find something new
    to discover about one another.
May each day bring you
even more reasons
    to cherish each other.
Together, may you create the kind
    of memories that last a lifetime.
More than anything else, may you
    carry this spirit of love
through every season and
    on through the years,
and may it brighten each day
    of your lives.

— Edmund O'Neill

Marriage Is like
a Patchwork Quilt...

Life and marriage are like
a patchwork quilt.
Each one has to start with
a small beginning.
By itself it has no meaning
or companionship.
But as each piece is added
it becomes more beautiful
and interesting.

Each piece does not have to
be perfect because that is
what makes it unique.
And even if it isn't just
the right size or shape,
by working together
it will finally fit in.
And when you come to the end
and look at it as a whole,
all the perfect and imperfect pieces
have turned into one beautiful gift.

— Connie R. Carter

A Wife Is...

Your truest friend and confidante.
She is laughter in the night
and joy in the morning.
She is tender touches, loving smiles,
a wonderful heart.

She is the dearest person you know,
the one who is closest to your dreams
and nearest to all that is meaningful.
She is a precious part of your life,
a vital connection to every tomorrow.
With her you feel important,
needed, accepted.
She is warm sunshine on a cloudy day
and love's celebration of all that is good.
She is...
a wife.

— L. E. Knight

What Is a Husband?

A husband is a man
who overlooks your bad points,
but doesn't overlook you.
He's someone who can
make you feel beautiful
by a look in his eyes.
He knows when to wrap his arms
around you
to shield you from the world,
and when to leave you alone
if you need some space.
He gives you the freedom
to be your own person,
but is always available
so that you're never alone.
A husband shares what goes on
in his life
and cares about what goes on in yours.
He's a part of you;
he's always on your mind
and in your heart.
A husband is an irreplaceable
person in your life —
he's a lover, a protector,
a companion, and a friend.

— Barbara Cage

As You Walk Through Your Life Together...

Remember that the first step
begins any journey...
setting the course,
mapping out your future,
choosing the direction you will follow
as husband and wife.

Remember that each road,
no matter how straight it seems,
has bumps and detours.
No matter how perfect your plans are laid,
the course can change
when you least expect it.
But whatever bump or hill or detour
you experience on your journey,
it will only enhance the trip.

Do not be stopped by a change in plans.
Remember that a delay
can offer a chance to explore territory
you might not otherwise have seen.

The best part of the trip is the journey,
not the destination.

So with the keys to each other's
heart in hand,
may your road to happiness
and a successful life together begin
with the first step as you wed,
and may every road you follow
lead you to another memory.

— Linda Robertson

True Love Is
"We" Instead of "Me"

True love is being the best of friends — being able to say and share anything while still being sensitive to the other's feelings.

It is built upon complete trust — complete by knowing that you can never be deceitful or misleading, because to do so would forever cloud the relationship with doubt.

True love is knowing that you'd rather be with this other person than with anyone else, and you feel a sense of emptiness when the two of you are apart.

It's when you always think of the future in terms of "we" instead of "me."

True love is treasuring the touch of the other person while feeling a sense of contentment and completeness as you emotionally and physically embrace.

True love is wanting to make the
other person happy and fulfilled in every
possible way while doing everything you
can to prevent their distress.

It is a commitment to working out
the differences that will always come
about when two people become one.

It is knowing that life will bring pain
and sorrow, but together, you will
support each other and overcome even
the most difficult times.

True love is showing and saying
"I love you" even when you both know —
through a simple smile — that doing
so isn't necessary.

True love is complete within itself,
and it lasts into eternity.

— Tim Tweedie

Remember What's Most Important...

Preserve sacredly
the privacies of your home,
your married state
and your heart.

With mutual help
build your quiet world.
Let moments of alienation,
if they occur, be healed at once.
To each other confess
and all will come out right.
Never let the morrow's sun
still find you at variance.
Renew and renew your vow.
It will do you good;
and thereby your minds
will grow together
contented in that love
which is stronger than death,
and you will be truly one.

— Margaret Springdale

Promises to Keep

o treat each other with respect
and kindness.
To be open-minded, so that you may
see each other's point of view.
To listen to your heart and with your heart.
To be patient when things don't go right;
eventually, they'll be replaced
by good things.
To be loving, especially when the other
is hurting over something.
To be honest and don't hold back
your feelings.
To laugh a lot at yourselves and
with each other.
To enjoy the good times, and think of them
more often than the bad ones.
To be there for one another at all times.
To make yourself, as well as your spouse,
happy, and let them find
their own happiness, too.
To share all things; learn new things.
To always remember the times
when you first fell in love
and all the special moments.
To keep making every year special,
and always love one another.

— Carol Howard

The Five Foundations of a Happy Marriage

1) Don't expect your mate to read your mind. Be a willing, open communicator. Don't ever be afraid to share your feelings (especially the good ones).

2) Keep romance alive. Love notes, flowers, candy, dating, cuddling, and any unexpected acts of kindness all go a long way to keeping the romance in any relationship. Think of ways to show you are in love, and do them.

3) Have a sense of humor. And have fun. Remember the things you like to do together, find some more, and then do them. Laughing and having a good time together is one of the best ways to stay happy and fulfilled.

4) Have an adjustable attitude. Attitude works wonders on bad days and situations. Whether it's seeing the humor in a situation, making a change, or accepting something, attitude is one of the greatest forces in life. Always remember that you can control yours.

5) Love each other unconditionally and always. Love others. Love nature. Appreciate the little things; stop to enjoy a sunset or the smell of a flower. Look for the happiness and the good in life, and your life will be happy and good, too.

— Barbara Cage

Love Is at Its Best
When It Is Given Completely...

When you walk hand in hand
with the person of your dreams
When you talk into the wee hours
of the morning —
sharing your most intimate thoughts
and dreams
When you kiss each other's lips
as delicately as the petals
of the pinkest rose
When the darkest nights
turn into the brightest mornings
as you're held in each other's arms

When the tickle of a whisper in the ear
is as warm as the breath of a fire
When you see endless color and passion
in each other's eyes
When the sweetest embrace between you
touches the depths of your souls

— Mark V. Marino

Marriage Is Two People
Sharing Everything in Life

In marriage
two people share
all their dreams and goals
their weaknesses and strengths
In marriage
two people share
all the joys and sadnesses of life
and all the supreme pleasures
In marriage
two people share
all of their emotions and feelings
all of their tears and laughter

Marriage is the most
fulfilling relationship
one can have
and the love that you share
as husband and wife
is beautifully forever

— Susan Polis Schutz

When You Enter
The World of Marriage...

After the rice is thrown and the tuxedos are returned. After the thank-you cards are sent and the florist is paid in full. After the sunburn from your honeymoon starts to heal and the great photo of the wedding party slips into a frame. Then it can begin.

When the quiet settles around the two of you and it's no longer about fine tuning the details of the event. When the phone rings less often and the mail begins to slow. When saying the words "husband" and "wife" no longer seems strange off the tongue.

When it starts to be about watching
old movies together at two o'clock
in the morning and grabbing him
to slow dance while he shaves. When
it's no longer about picking out china
patterns, but rather about picking
out food to put on them. When it's
taking the car in for an oil change or
fixing a favorite meal simply because
it's Tuesday.

When you argue over money and
make up over ice-cream cones in
the park. When you hear his key
click in the front door and it brings
a smile to your lips. When you
cuddle at night before the dreams
come. When the world looks at the
two of you but only sees a couple.
Then, at that moment, hand in
hand, the two of you leave the
wedding behind and enter the world
of marriage.

— Michelle Mariotti

Together

You and I by this lamp with these
Few books shut out the world. Our knees
Touch almost in this little space.
But I am glad. I see your face.
The silences are long, but each
Hears the other without speech.
And in this simple scene there is
The essence of all subtleties,
The freedom from all fret and smart,
The one sure sabbath of the heart.

The world — we cannot conquer it,
Nor change the minds of fools one whit.
Here, here alone do we create
Beauty and peace inviolate;
Here night by night and hour by hour
We build a high impregnable tower
Whence may shine, now and again,
A light to light the feet of men
When they see the rays thereof:
And this is marriage, this is love.

— Ludwig Lewisohn

Poem for an Anniversary

All the roads we've traveled down,
all the times we've turned around.
All the smiles and memories
and times we just got through.
All the wonder of the days,
all the many different ways
we learned how "together"
works through change
and unexpected moves.
The milestones come and go
in life;
we ride through doubts,
we hold on tight
to what we know
and whom we love
and this-is-where-we-are.
Who would have thought
we'd come this far
still following each other's star
with friends to celebrate the journey:
with love,
and all these years.

— Ashley Rice

Will You Love Me
When I'm Old?

would ask of you, my darling,
A question soft and low,
That gives me many a heartache
As the moments come and go.

Your love I know is truthful,
    But the truest love grows cold;
It is this that I would ask you:
    Will you love me when I'm old?

Life's morn will soon be waning,
    And its evening bells be tolled,
But my heart shall know no sadness,
    If you love me when I'm old.

Down the stream of life together
    We are sailing side by side,
Hoping some bright day to anchor
    Safe beyond the surging tide.
Today our sky is cloudless,
    But the night may clouds unfold;
But, though storms may gather round us,
    Will you love me when I'm old?

When my hair shall shade the snowdrift,
    And mine eyes shall dimmer grow,
I would lean upon some loved one,
    Through the valley as I go.
I would claim of you a promise,
    Worth to me a world of gold;
It is only this, my darling,
    That you'll love me when I'm old.

                        — Author Unknown

Marriage Can Hold
Everlasting Love

ind happiness each day
in the love you give each other.
Take time to share words, touches,
and quiet moments that say
you'll always care.
Make each day the kind of day
you shared
when you first fell in love.
Let love take you to the mountaintops
and carry you gently through the valleys.
Always remember the sweetness
of sharing,
the need for confiding, the reasons for caring.
Keep learning all you can about each other;
you might be surprised by how much more
you'll find to love.

When words are few and far between,
   hold hands and let love fill the silence.
Follow your dreams, walking hand in hand,
and you'll see the world around you
   become a wonderland.
Take good care of one another
and you'll find that love will care
for both of you.
Never forget that marriage is making home
out of any place you go
and finding joy in any kind of weather.
Welcome each day with a loving hug
   and a kiss,
and share a life of happiness.

— Deborah Lawson

Keep Your Love Growing

Keep your dreams close at heart,
keep your arms close to touch,
and keep sharing happy times together.
Keep enjoying each other,
keep the smiles coming,
and keep rediscovering
this wonderful love you share.
Keep counting your blessings,
keep the magic alive in your hearts.
Keep reaching out,
keep listening,
and keep being the very best of friends.
Keep your love growing, and
keep wishing on a star.

— Linda E. Knight

You Have a Lifetime to Share... but Take It One Day at a Time

In your hands, you have the keys
to a beautiful, fulfilling future;
you can get there together
by relying on each other for
all the important things you need,
and by blending your individual strengths
and talents
into a beautiful union that will last
all the days of your lives.

In your hearts, you have
the greatest blessing
anyone ever receives:
love that can last forever.
Cherish your love as a miracle,
and always appreciate
the gift you have in each other.

— Edmund O'Neill

Keep Your Commitment Strong

I n everyone's life
there are problems to solve.
Even in the strongest relationship,
there are differences to overcome.
It is easy to give up when confronted
with difficulties;
to fool yourself into believing that
perfection can be found somewhere else.
But true happiness and a lasting
relationship are found
when you look inside yourself for
solutions to the problems.
Instead of walking away when things
get tough and blaming the other person,
look for compromise and forgiveness.
Caring is not a matter of convenience.
It is a commitment of one soul to another.
And if each gives generously of themselves,
then both lives are enriched.
The problems will come and go,
just like the changing seasons.
But unselfish love is constant
and everlasting.

— Susan Staszewski

Even the Best Relationships Need to Remember This...

If you can always find time to talk it out,
if you can listen with your hearts,
if you can open up doors that
   sometimes get closed off to your
   innermost feelings,
if you can be gentle,
if you can be strong,
if you can walk the unknown journey
   and always take one another along,
if you can help each other over the rises,
if you can understand any tears that fall,
if you can build the bridges that will take
   you over the highest walls,
if you can go to the special places
   where the most perfect truth exists...

You will discover that love
will always be
the best thing that there is.

— Collin McCarty

Any Wife or Husband

 et us be guests in one another's house
With deferential "No" and courteous "Yes";
Let us take care to hide our foolish moods
Behind a certain show of cheerfulness.

Let us avoid all sullen silences;
We should find fresh and sprightly things
    to say;
I must be fearful lest you find me dull,
And you must dread to bore me any way.

Let us knock gently at each other's heart,
Glad of a chance to look within — and yet
Let us remember that to force one's way
Is the unpardoned breach of etiquette.

So shall I be hostess — you, the host —
Until all need for entertainment ends;
We shall be lovers when the last door shuts,
But what is better still — we shall be friends.

— Carol Haynes

Always Build
"A Bridge Instead of a Wall"

hey say a wife and husband, bit by bit,
    Can rear between their lives
        a mighty wall,
So thick they cannot
        talk with ease through it,
Nor can they see across,
        it stands so tall!
Its nearness frightens them but each alone
        Is powerless to tear its bulk away,
And each, dejected, wishes he had known
        For such a wall,
            some magic thing to say.
So let us build with master art, my dear,
        A bridge of faith between
            your life and mine,
A bridge of tenderness and very near
        A bridge of understanding,
            strong and fine —
Till we have formed
        so many lovely ties
There will never be room
        for walls to rise!

               — Author Unknown

Never Forget
the Power of Love

Love is the most incredible
of all the experiences
that touch our lives.
It creates for us the world
    that we want to live in.
From the beginning of our lives,
we know that love is the power
that comforts and protects us;
it is the one feeling
that we can depend upon
    to help us through
life's ups and downs.
Love is the understanding
    and security that never changes;
it allows us to be ourselves
and feel self-confident.

As the two of you join together
and commit your love to each other,
remember the lessons of love
that you have always known.
Let your love comfort, support,
    and encourage you.
Let your love be the best part
    of your lives;
always know that it will make
    everything better,
and it will make your world
    a place of happiness.

— Dena Dilaconi

Motto for a
Great Marriage

A great marriage begins with two people in love with each other, loving each other with all their hearts... unconditionally, deeply, crazily, wonderfully, sweetly, madly, freely. They think about sharing forever together, supporting each other's dreams, making plans to walk together as one, yet keeping and enhancing their own identities.

A great marriage is made up of two people who practice showing their love the way they show it best, the way that brings out the best in each other. They listen to each other as they would listen to a friend because in so many great marriages, the two people are best friends.

They learn from their mistakes and find ways to communicate their concerns, share their feelings, and manage their differences. They make the success of their marriage a priority and keep their marriage new and interesting.

Partners in great marriages have a sacred contract. They are settled in their commitment to love, cherish, and care for their love and their marriage, and they do what they need to do to keep it strong through sickness and health, poverty and wealth, and all the in-betweens. They choose to solve their problems in a spirit of cooperation with each other, assuming an attitude of togetherness, not separation. They forgive each other. They are loyal to each other. They treat each other as sweethearts.

Great marriages begin and end with love. They never give up, no matter what, and love anyway... always.

— Donna Fargo

A Recipe for Everlasting Love

(Serves two people generously)

Directions:

Take two compatible souls and add a teaspoon of passion and intimacy. Remember to sprinkle in a dash of trust and honesty during the initial stages. Sift in a layer of compassion and reliability, then mix with an ounce of understanding and patience.

While stirring, add a cup of consistency. Swirl gently, and fill in the gaps with a smidgen of communication and tolerance. Thoroughly coat with unselfishness, and sprinkle with kindness and humor.

Leave to warm in the moderate sun over a lengthy period of time. Best served with a spice of devotion and a pinch of loyalty.

— Benjamin Raymond

In the Garden of Love and Marriage

he greatest earthly blessing is to find the right person in this vast world, fall in love, and marry.

The second greatest blessing is to take your marriage and nourish the love within, watching it grow around both of you like a beautiful garden, sheltering you from the pressures that can weaken your love.

Even in marriage, you need to be diligent gardeners — planting your love firmly in honesty and respect, cultivating communication and understanding, and watering often with generous amounts of romance and excitement.

From your caring, you will both harvest an abundance of happiness and peace that few people ever possess.

May your garden together forever display the beauty that your hearts hold for each other.

— Tim Tweedie

A Happy Marriage Is like a Flower...

The more it's cared for,
the brighter it blooms.
Each year that you celebrate
   your marriage
is a reminder of your deep commitment
   to the vows that sealed your love.
The way you complement each other
   is truly a gift to be treasured.
Not everyone is so lucky to find
   a soul mate
to journey through life with
   "for richer or poorer"
      and "in sickness and in health."

— Elizabeth Hornsey Reeves

The Magical Journey of Marriage

You wait a long time for the right person to come into your life. When it happens, magic begins. A special bond is forged. It's the two of you against the world. You halve each other's sorrow and double each other's joy. Together, you tackle any problem and reach for any goal.

Marriage is much more than a wonderful destination. It's a magical journey full of hope, friendship, romance, laughter, and love that the two of you travel hand in hand each day of your lives. Your marriage is a journey so precious and unique that no one else can even hope to understand it.

May the wonder and magic of your journey together be a never-ending fairy tale.

— Donna Gephart

The Art of Marriage

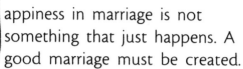

appiness in marriage is not something that just happens. A good marriage must be created. In the art of marriage the *little things* are the *big things*...

It is never being too old to hold hands.

It is remembering to say, "I love you," at least once each day.

It is never going to sleep angry.

It is at no time taking the other for granted; the courtship shouldn't end with the honeymoon, it should continue through all the years.

It is having a mutual sense of values and common objectives; it is standing together facing the world.

It is forming a circle of love that gathers in the whole family.

It is doing things for each other, not in the attitude of duty or sacrifice, but in the spirit of joy.

It is speaking words of appreciation and demonstrating gratitude in thoughtful ways.

It is not expecting the husband to wear a halo or the wife to have the wings of an angel. It is not looking for perfection in each other. It is cultivating flexibility, patience, understanding and a sense of humor.

It is having the capacity to forgive and forget.

It is giving each other an atmosphere in which each can grow.

It is finding room for the things of the spirit. It is a common search for the good and the beautiful.

It is not only marrying the right partner, it is *being* the right partner.

It is discovering what marriage can be, at its best, as expressed in the words Mark Twain used in a tribute to his wife: "Wherever she was, there was Eden."

— Wilferd A. Peterson

Love

To renounce your individuality,
to see with another's eyes,
to hear with another's ears,
To be two and yet one,
to so melt and mingle
that you no longer know
you are you or another,
To constantly absorb and
constantly radiate,
To reduce earth, sea and sky
and all that in them is
to a single being so wholly
that nothing whatever is withheld,
To be prepared at any moment for sacrifice,
To double your personality in bestowing it —
that is love.

— Théophile Gautier

Forever

How can you ever explain
some of the deepest feelings
you've ever felt for someone?

You try to tell them with words
that speak of joy and gratitude
and so much love;
You try to show them with touches,
with smiles chasing away the tears,
with little caresses that say you care,
with secret intimacies you share.

You make the most of each day together;
You take the time to make your love
the best it can possibly be.
You do whatever you can
and whatever it takes, and you hope
that their heart understands
what your heart is trying to say
when it says...
"I love you,
and I know
I'll always feel that way."

— Collin McCarty

Marriage Joins Two People in the Circle of Its Love

arriage is a commitment to life — to the best that two people can find and bring out in each other. It offers opportunities for sharing and growth no other human relationship can equal, a physical and emotional joining that is promised for a lifetime.

Within the circle of its love, marriage encompasses all of life's most important relationships. A wife and husband are each other's best friend, confidant, lover, teacher, listener, and critic. There may come times when one partner is heartbroken or ailing, and the love of the other may resemble the tender caring of a parent for a child.

Marriage deepens and enriches every
facet of life. Happiness is fuller; memories
are fresher; commitment is stronger; even
anger is felt more strongly, and passes away
more quickly.

Marriage understands and forgives the
mistakes life is unable to avoid. It encourages
and nurtures new life, new experiences,
and new ways of expressing love through the
seasons of life.

When two people pledge to love and care
for each other in marriage, they create a spirit
unique to themselves, which binds them closer
than any spoken or written words. Marriage
is a promise, a potential, made in the hearts
of two people who love, which takes a lifetime
to fulfill.

— Edmund O'Neill

Together in Marriage...

Together in marriage
you will bring out the best
in each other
You will learn from each other
and grow from your differences
You will be two individuals
living your own lives
with each other as one

Together in marriage
you will be stronger
more sensitive
more aware, more knowing
and more at peace
than you are individually
You will be better people

Together in marriage
your love will give understanding
to all that you do
because you will share
your ideas, goals
and frustrations
And you will always have
someone to support
whatever you say and do

Together in marriage
you will be able
to achieve
all that you want
in life

— Susan Polis Schutz

You Share
the Greatest Gift

arriage is a gift
sealed with the promise
to love and cherish always.
Through time and memory,
may your love stand tall
like a beacon.
Take special care in celebrating
and cherishing the one
whom your heart loves.
Through all the seasons of life,
share your joys and sorrows
freely and openly.
In victory and defeat,
failure and success,
be there for one another
to listen, care, and support.
Remember that the realities of life
make us or break us.
Hold your love gently, guard it carefully,
and celebrate it always.
May the love you share always be
a welcome place to come home to.

— Linda E. Knight

Between Husband and Wife... "You Are the Love Song of My Life"

here would be no song without
lyrics and a pretty melody
Like there would be no marriage
without the love between
a husband and a wife
Together we make the music that
my soul needs to hear
You are the love song of my life

Each verse of life gets better
as we write our own story
Our hopes and dreams keep close harmony
against the sounds of strife
The cadence of the rhythms blends body,
mind, and soul together
You are the love song of my life

We make music we can dance to as we
hold each other close
To feel the other's love is the dream of
every husband, every wife
We sing our song together, inspired by
blessed happiness
You are the love song of my life

— Donna Fargo

The Promises of Marriage

Marriage is a promise of companionship,
of having someone to share
all of life's experiences.
Marriage does not promise that there will
not be any rough times,
just the assurance that there will
always be someone
who cares and will help you through
to better times.
Marriage does not promise eternal romance,
just eternal love and commitment.
Marriage can't prevent disappointments,
disillusionment, or grief,
but it can offer hope, acceptance,
and comfort.

Marriage can't protect you from making
  individual choices
  or shelter you from the world,
  but it will help to reassure you
  that there is someone by your side
  who truly cares.
  When the world hurts you
  and makes you feel vulnerable,
  marriage offers the promise that there will
  be someone waiting to listen,
  to console, to inspire.
Marriage is the joining of two people
  who share the promise
  that only marriage can make —
  to share the sunshine and the shadows,
  and to experience a richer, more fulfilling life
  because of it.

— Bettie Meeks

Marriage Is like a River

wo strong rivers flow swift and sure
on parallel courses through life's
toughest terrain.
One crashes and rushes on its way;
the other meanders and winds
  on a languid course.
At one point, by God's design, they merge;
each one lends itself to the whole.
The waters, blending and churning,
create a mightier river together
than they ever could apart.
So it is with marriage, as well.
Two souls bring their strengths, weaknesses,
similarities, and differences together,
balancing each other as no others could.
In this way, they become like the river:
in the worst of times, they find the strength
  to carve through mountains,
and in the best of times, they find
the devotion to forge new paths
through an uncharted paradise
that only they can share.

— Judy Edwards

How to Make a Marriage Last Forever

1. Remember that the love you share is holy — set aside from the rest of the world as a perfect union.

2. Be best friends. Listen to each other. Offer praise. Be considerate. Think carefully before criticizing. Put each other first.

3. Be intimate and caring. Be frivolous and daring. Be sure to make a special moment every day.

In other words...
keep the magic;
keep the friendship;
keep the love you share as sacred
and above all other things this
world can offer.
For nothing is more beautiful than
the miracle of marriage. Its beauty
lasts a lifetime when two people
care so much that they love each
other forever.

— Regina Hill

May You Always Be Happy!

We are not meant to go through life alone.
We need a partner who will
forever remain by our side —
someone to lean on at times,
remembering, as well,
that we will be leaned on, too.

In marriage, your partner
will share your joy
and hold you in sorrow.
Understand that there will be difficult times
and doubt may cloud your lives.
It is then that you must
trust each other the most
and believe that love will sustain you.

Do not give up easily;
fight for what is most precious —
your marriage.
Help it survive
by nurturing it every single day.
Never hesitate to say, "I love you,"
or to be the first one to say, "I'm sorry."
Give a lot,
overlook even more,
and always expect as much in return.
Never look back
or lose yourself,
but celebrate the special privilege
of being a couple.
Never lose sight
of what brought you to the altar
in the first place:
your special love for each other.
Cherish that always.
May you find nothing but happiness
as you share the wonderful world
of marriage.

— Linda Hersey

ACKNOWLEDGMENTS

We gratefully acknowledge the permission granted by the following authors, publishers, and authors' representatives to reprint poems or excerpts from their publications.

Barbara Cage for "May Your Marriage Be Blessed with Love, Friendship, and Faith." Copyright © 2002 by Barbara Cage. All rights reserved.

Connie R. Carter for "Marriage Is like a Patchwork Quilt...." Copyright © 2002 by Connie R. Carter. All rights reserved.

Michelle Mariotti for "When You Enter the World of Marriage...." Copyright © 2002 by Michelle Mariotti. All rights reserved.

Deborah Lawson for "Marriage Can Hold Everlasting Love." Copyright © 2002 by Deborah Lawson. All rights reserved.

Linda E. Knight for "Keep Your Love Growing" and "You Share the Greatest Gift." Copyright © 2002 by Linda E. Knight. All rights reserved.

PrimaDonna Entertainment Corp. for "Motto for a Great Marriage" and "Between Husband and Wife... 'You Are the Love Song of My Life'" by Donna Fargo. Copyright © 2002 by PrimaDonna Entertainment Corp. All rights reserved.

Benjamin Raymond for "A Recipe for Everlasting Love." Copyright © 2002 by Benjamin Raymond. All rights reserved.

Tim Tweedie for "In the Garden of Love and Marriage." Copyright © 2002 by Tim Tweedie. All rights reserved.

Elizabeth Hornsey Reeves for "A Happy Marriage Is like a Flower." Copyright © 2002 by Elizabeth Hornsey Reeves. All rights reserved.

Donna Gephart for "The Magical Journey of Marriage." Copyright © 2002 by Donna Gephart. All rights reserved.

Heacock Literary Agency for "The Art of Marriage" from THE ART OF LIVING by Wilferd A. Peterson, published by Galahad Books. Copyright © 1960, 1961, 1962, 1963, 1966 by Wilferd A. Peterson. All rights reserved.

Judy Edwards for "Marriage Is like a River." Copyright © 2002 by Judy Edwards. All rights reserved.

A careful effort has been made to trace the ownership of selections used in this anthology in order to obtain permission to reprint copyrighted material and give proper credit to the copyright owners. If any error or omission has occurred, it is completely inadvertent, and we would like to make corrections in future editions provided that written notification is made to the publisher:

BLUE MOUNTAIN ARTS, INC., P.O. Box 4549, Boulder, Colorado 80306.